WILLS

of
Berkeley County
West Virginia

and
Other Estate Documents

An Index: 1744-1880

ORIGINALLY PUBLISHED BY TRACES

Compiled by
Dale Walton Morrow and
Deborah Jensen Morrow

HERITAGE BOOKS
2008

HERITAGE BOOKS
AN IMPRINT OF HERITAGE BOOKS, INC.

Books, CDs, and more—Worldwide

For our listing of thousands of titles see our website
at
www.HeritageBooks.com

Published 2008 by
HERITAGE BOOKS, INC.
Publishing Division
100 Railroad Ave. #104
Westminster, Maryland 21157

Other books by the authors:

Distribution of Estate Accounts, Washington County, Maryland, 1778-1835

Marriages of Washington County, Maryland: An Index, 1799-1860

Washington County, Maryland Cemetery Records: Volumes 1-7
Dale Walton Morrow

Wills of Jefferson County, West Virginia, 1801-1899

Wills of Washington County, [Maryland], 1776-1890

International Standard Book Numbers
Paperbound: 978-1-58549-246-6
Clothbound: 978-0-7884-7235-0

INTRODUCTION

Berkeley County, Virginia, now West Virginia, was formed in 1772 from the parent county of Frederick. Berkeley County became a part of West Virginia in 1863, during the Civil War, when the new state was formed from the parent state of Virginia.

ENTRIES/SYMBOLS

The surnames are indexed alphabetically, followed by individual given names. The symbols are as follows:

- w - indicates a will.
- f - indicates an account such as an inventory, estate, sale, etc. Each "f" stands for one document.

BELL, James wff1824 - indicates a will and two other estate documents relating to this name dated 1824.

LOST WILL BOOKS

If the reader should locate a will or account in one of the following books: 11, 16, 18, 19, or 20, note that these books are unaccounted for and all documents therein have been lost.

To inquire about specific documents and current copying charges, the reader should write to the Clerk's Office, Berkeley County Courthouse, Martinsburg, West Virginia 25401.

BESHEAR, Zephruial wf1795; f1803; f1805
BESORE, Barury w1795
BETTY (BEATTY?), William fff1829
BIDLER, Jacob f1795
BILLINGSBY, Charles wf1805
BILLIP, John w1774
BILLMYER (BILLMIRE, BILLMYRE), Conrad (&
   heirs) f1848
   Jacob f1829
   James M. f1848
   Jane ff1871
   John w1861
   Margaret w1838
   Mary E. f1848
   Michael f1874; f1877; f1875
   Susan J. f1848
BINGERMAN, Henry wf1774
BISHOP, Greenbury f1812; f1818; f1827
   Jacob fff1824; f1828; f1829; f1832;
   f1838
BITZER, Michael wf1817
BIVENS, William f1812
BLACKFORD, Benjamin f1781
   Ebenezer f1793; f1795
BLACKMORE , No name ff1803
   James f1788
   John f1793
   Lawrence f1793
   Lawrence O. ff1795
   Lawrence Owen fffff1805
BLUE, Catherine f1795
   John f1795
   Uriah f1793; f1812
BOAK, John f1818
   Robert f1829
BOAKE, John ff1812; f1817
BOARMAN, Charles w1879
BODINE, Richard ff1874
BOGGS, James f1803; f1805
   William wf1788; wf1832
BOHERT, Martin w1788
BOLEY, Benjamin f1795; ff1868
   Simon wf1781
BOOTH, Caleb fff1817
BOSWELL, Walter wf1774
BOWERS, Ann f1871
   Catherine C. ff1871
   Elizabeth ff1838; f1841
   Frederick f1812
   George wf1805
   Henry w1788; wff1832
   William f1854
BOWLAND, Michael f1788
BOWMAN, Andrew f1803; f1805; f1817; f1824
   George ff1829; f1832

BOYD, Benjamin R. w1861
   E.H. w1838
   Elisha wf1838; f1841
   John wf1795; f1805
   Samuel w1817
   Sarah wffff1805
   Thomas f1788
   William wf1774; f1795
BOYER, John A. f1877
BOYLE, Henry f1805
   John w1854
BOYLES, Henry f1793
BRANNON, Elizabeth w1861
   Isaac f1817
   John f1817
BRATT, Arthur M. f1871; ff1874
BRENNER, Frederick ff1838; f1841
   Susan w1844; ff1847
BRINDLE, Mary w1879
BRISCOE (BISCOE), Doctor f1803
   James w1774
   John wf1788; f1805; f1812
   Thomas w1878
BROOK, William w1795; ff1803
BROOKS, Samuel wf1788
   William f1812
BROSIUS, John Andrew f1805
BROUSE, Andrew w1805
BROWN, Archibald f1774
   Elizabeth f1841
   James w1774; w1841; f1844
   John w1795
   Joseph S. f1874
   Margaret f1848
   Martin Sr. f1877
   Perry f1868
   Thomas f1848
   William wf1795; w1841
BRYANS, John T. fff1832
BRYARLY, Ann w1824
   Richard w1828
   Robert P. f1871
   Thomas w1848
   Thomas C. f1848
BURGHILL, William f1795
BUCKLES, Abraham f1774; wfff1838; f1841
   Dr. E.G. ff1877
   James w1795
   John ff1812
   Lewis M. fff1844
   Mary w1774
   Robert w1788; f1795; f1817
BUCKS, Robert ff1805
BUEURR, Gasper f1774
BULL, Robert wf1805
BUNN, Benjamin f1805

CHIDESTER, Peter D. fff1828
CHRISTIE, Robert ff1847
CHRISTY, Adam w1812
    Robert w1832
    Samuel fff1807
    William w1854
CHRONISTER, C. f1868
CLAGET, Richard fff1828; 1829
CLARE, George w1829
CLARK, Elizabeth w1772
    Joseph f1812
    Walter ff1785
CLAUSON, Richard w1776
CLAWSON, Isaac ff1823; f1826
    John wff1812; f1821
CLAYCOMB, Conrad f1782; w1839; fff1841
    Mary fff1841
CLEMENS, Leonard f1826
    Robert f1826
CLEMMENS, Margaret w1849
CLISE, Jacob ff1795
COCKBURN, Robert Sr. wf1821
COFFENBERGER, George fff1847
    George Lewis wf1812
    George L. ff1821; f1823
COFFMAN, Jacob f1785; f1789
    John f1776
COLBERT, Fielding w1854; f1860; ff1868
COLE, Jacob f1788
    William w1785
COLLET, Moser wf1782
COLLIER, Daniel ff1868
    David w1861
COLLINS, James fff1873
    Moses ff1817
COLSTON, Edward w1854
    Elizabeth w1849
    John M. w1825
    Lucy Ann f1874; f1878
    Rawleigh w1823; f1826; f1825; f1828
COLVIN, Thomas f1812
COMEGGS, Jacob f1805; ff1807
    Benjamin w1854
COMPTON, Elijah ff1817
    Isaac f1825
CONELEY, Benjamin w1841
CONGLE, John f1782
CONNELLY, Jenkins f1785; f1791
    Lawrence f1795
CONLEY, David f1849
CONRAD, D.H. ff1874; f1878;w1877
COOK, Benjamin w1861
    Giles w1795
COOKUS, Henry w1776; f1785; w1789
    Mortimer f1868
COON, Adam f1789; f1795
COONTZ, William w1785

COOPER, Adam f1776
    Alexander w1849
    Hazlett w1785
    Isaac f1795
    Maria w1855; ff1868
    Ruth wfff1849
COPENHAVER, Michael w1785; ff1785
CORNELIUS, Samuel ff1861
COUCH, Rebecca f1832
COUCHMAN, Benedict ff1795
    Catherine ff1807
    Elizabeth f1795; w1864; ff1873;
        f1874; fff1878
    George fff1832
    H.J. ff1849
    Henry wff1847
    Henry C. w1849
    Henry G. f1868
    James H. w1862
    John G. ff1878
    Mary E. f1871
    Michael fff1841
    Sara O. f1871
    Mrs. Susannah wfff1849
COULTER, Rebecca f1823
COUN, James wf1795
COUNCLIN, John w1795
COVENHAVER, William wfff1832
COWNOVER, Eliza f1828
COX, Ann Virginia f1847; f1849
    Henry f1829
    Horace f1841; ff1845
    Jacob ff1864; f1868
COZZEUS, Ann ff1878
CRAGG, Jonathan f1795
CRAIGHILL, Elizabeth wff1823
    John B. w1807; f1823; f1825
CRAIGHTON, John f1782
CRANE, James f1785; w1795
CRASS, Basil fff1823
CRASSON, Elanor w1823; ff1825
CREAMER, John ff1812
CREIGHTON, Robert wff1795
CRIM, George fffff1871; f1874
CRISWELL, Abraham f1832; ff1838; ff1839
    Agnes fff1849
    Elizabeth f1849
    Elizabeth A. f1852
    Elizabeth Ann f1841; f1845
    J.W. f1841
    John fffff1832; f1839; f1849
    John J. f1839
    John W. f1845; ff1849
    Rebecca f1841

4

MWELL, John C. f1823; f1826; f1832
   Philonius f1874
OK(S), Eliza f1841
   Jacob ff1795; ff1805; f1807
THERS, George ff1807
   John ff1805
   Mary f1805
UCH, Rebecca w1826
W, John wf1772
   John R. w1861; f1871; f1872
   Sarah f1873
WEL, Henry f1807
WL, J.T. f1874
   John T. ff1874
   John f1849
   Peter w1852
   Sarah f1874
WLY, William f1795
M, Diana f1868
   George f1854
   John W. f1854
MLEY, Adam f1776
   John ff1812
   William wf1785
NINGHAM, Charity Ann f1847
   David f1874
   George f1776; ff1789; w1807; ff1812;
      f1828
   Hugh wf1817; f1821
   James wff1772
   John ffff1832; ff1837
   John W. f1847
   M.E.N. f1874
   Margaret f1871
   Margaret M. f1864
   Martha J. f1864; f1871
   Mary E.N. f1871
   Mary Emma f1864
   Peter w1877
   Robert w1782
   Ruth ff1812; f1828
   Samuel w1823; f1832
   Samuel A. f1845; f1849
   Susan f1847
   William wf1785; wf1854; f1861;w1862;
      f1874
   William D. f1864
   William Jr. ff1864
TIS, George H. f1864; f1868
   Jacob f1852; f1854
   Job wff1795; f1805
   William ff1829
HWA, Aaron D. f1841
   Catherine f1849; w1854
   D.M. f1841
   David f1849
   David M. fff1832; ff1845; f1849

   David Nall f1841
   Heirs f1849
   John fff1823; f1826
   John D. w1879
   Jonathan wfff1832; f1838; f1839
   Mary f1841
CUSHWA, Mary A. f1849
   Mary A.T. f1849
   Mary S. f1845
   Peter w1839

DAILEY, John f1849, f1854
   John W. f1874
DALRYMPLE, John wf1772
DALWICK, John w1861
DANDRIDGE, Alexander Spottswood wf1772
DANIEL, Ann f1841
   Elizabeth w1796
   John f1795; f1805
   Robert f1841; f1854; ff1874
   Robert Sr. wf1822
DAUGHERTY (DOUGHERTY), Alexander wf1837;
      f1841
   Elizabeth I. f1841
   Hugh w1827
   James w1822
   Mary w1824; f1827
DAVENPORT, Abraham w1789
   Braxton w1861
   Marmaduke f1772
DAVIDSON, Mary S. f1807
DAVIS, Daniel fff1772; w1795; ff1806;
      f1807
   Eleanor H. w1807
   George ff1874
   George W. f1874
   Jacob w1772
   John f1795; w1796
   Joseph wf1795
   William wf1772
DAWSON, Allen f1871
   Frederick f1795
   Jefferson f1871; ff1874
DAY, James W. ff1878
DECK, Nancy f1827
DEEL, Peter fff1806
DELBRIDGE, Eliza f1827
DEMIND, John f1789
DEMOSS, Charles w1772; f1796; fff1795
   Rebecca wf1789; f1795
   Thomas ff1795
DENNY, James H. w1861; ff1874
DENNISON, Thomas f1831
DENNY, Ann M. ff1871
DICK, Hannah f1772
DIEFFENDERFER (-DAFER), George Sr.
      w1831

DIXON, Thomas f1772
DOLL(DALL), Bernard wf1874; f1878
    C.S. f1841
    Catherine S. f1848
    Daniel H. f1871; ff1874
    E.S. f1841
    George f1871
    John f1837; f1842
    William H. f1871
DOOLEY, Samuel w1861
DORSEY, Edwin S. f1874
DOWLAN, Thomas wf1805
DOWNEY, Richard f1787; f1795
DOWNING, John f1848
    Talifaro f1849
DOWNS, Charles w1827
    Charles Sr. fff1829
    Henry w1807
DREW, William w1772; ff1796
DRINKER, Elizabeth w1854
    John w1824
DRISKELL (see O'DRISKELL)
DRISKELL, Patrick ff1842; f1848
DRUGGETT, Isaac fff1772
DUGAN, Frances R. f1861
    Francis R. w1849
    George H. ffff1831
DUFFY, Barney f1795; f1805
DUKE, John wwf1795
    Margaret w1789
    William f1795
DUNCAN, Mathew w1789
DUNHAM, Ben ff1837
    Benjamin f1841
    David f1841
    James fff1827
    Samuel fff1824; f1841
DUNN, William w1829
DURFINGER, Mary f1827
DUTTON, David w1837
DUVALL, Thomas f1871; ff1874

EACHS, Aaron f1853
EACUS, Newlin S. f1867
EADE, Robert f1778
EAKIN(S), Benjamin f1805
    Elizabeth fw1794
    James f1820; f1821
    Robert fw1817; f1820
    Thomas fw1794
EARLEY, Elizabeth fw1821
EBERSOLE, Emanuel w1826; f1829; f1831; f1839
EDDINS, Charles f1805; f1825
EDWARDS, Jonathan f1772
    Joseph w1794

EICHELBERGER, David f1829
ELLIOTT, Elijah f1829; f1849
    James f1805; f1811; f1817
ELLIS, Catherine Reed f1846; f1849; f1863
    Elenor f1805
    Elizabeth f1805; f1878
    Ellis w1831; f1839; f1846
    Enos fw1772
    Jacob f1817
    James w1805; fw1844; f1846
    John fw1772; fw1794; f1805; f1867;
        f1878
    John Denton f1846; f1849
    Laura B. f1878
    Mary Jane f1846; f1849; f1863
    Mordica f1772
    William fw1772
EMMERSON, Leonard f1825; f1826
EMMERT, George fw1821; f1826; f1829
    George C. f1844
    George E. f1839
ENGLE, William f1821
ENGLITH, Michael w1861
ENSMINGER, Charles w1861
    Christopher f1821; f1824; f1825
    Martin w1853
ENTLER, Adam fw1772; f1777
    Philip A. w1794
ETCHBERGER, Catherine E. f1878
    George P. f1867
EVANS, Allen M. w1853
    George F. f1867
    Isaac fw1778; f1825
    Isaac W. f1826; f1829
    J.T. f1867
    John fw1794; f1821; f1825; f1826; f18 ◄
    John (Jack) f1829
    Joseph fw1805
    Margaret f1811
    Mary f1839; f1844
    Sarah A. w1863
EVERHART, Henry w1861
    Nathan w1861; f1867
    Jacob f1846; f1849
EVERSON, Rosannah w1849
EWING, Thomas w1778; f1794; f1805

FARBER, Sebastian f1812
FARIS, Arthur f1810
FAUCK, Christopher w1812
    Jacob fff1812
FAULKNER, C.J. Jr. f1878
    James w1817; f1826; f1823; f1844
FEAMAN, Sarah wff1838
FELKER, John w1844
FELLER, Sarah f1829
FENIX, George ff1870
    George Jr. f1870

ELL, Benjamin f1849; f1853
  John f1849; f1853; f1868; f1870; f1873
  Nancy fff1868; f1874
IS, John w1861
ER, Catherine w1861
  S. w1844; f1849
DS, William wf1772
S, John w1831; f1838
  Thomas f1838; f1844; ff1854; f1868
R, Michael ff1829
ER, Eliza f1868
  Jacob wf1772; f1779
  James W.R. f1868
  Rachel Jane f1868
, Adam f1878
  Henry f1878
  Samuel f1874; w1877; f1878
KNER (FLECKNER), Peter ff1788
G, John M. f1853
  Josiah wf1849
  Thomas w1772
  Thomas G. w1878
CE, Jacob f1792
ING, Henry f1788; f1805
  John f1825; ff1826
MING, Sarah A. f1878
CHER, Azel ff1812; f1817; f1825; f1829
  David f1854; f1861
  John wfff1772
  Martha w1792
  Peter w1792; ff1805; f1808
  Sarah f1849
K, G. John f1792
E, George ff1812
ES, John ff1826
  George f1823
Y, Ann E. f1870; w1878
ES, John ff1838
ND, George f1788
K, Christopher f1826
  Elizabeth f1829
  Jacob ff1823
  Mary Ann f1829
, Christopher ff1812; f1817; f1823
  Elizabeth ff1825
, Henry fff1823; f1825; f1826
MAN, Elenor Virginia f1849
  James wf1831; f1844
AN, James F. wff1831
EST, Mary G. w1861
ER, Isaac f1788
  Thomas f1788; f1792
, Bryan f1772; f1788
NK, Barnard w1772
CEWAY, Joseph w1805; fff1810; ff1817;
  ff1823; f1829

FRAVEL, George f1870
  Mary f1870
FREDERICK, Henry f1772
FREEZE, Bernard fff1823
  John f1878
  Mary E. f1874; w1875; f1878
  Rose E. f1878
FRENCH, Catherine f1838; ff1839; f1844
  Henry f1838; f1839
  J.G. f1838
  Jacob ff1788; wf1826; f1828; f1838
  John f1831; ffff1838; f1844; f1849
  Mary fff1839; f1844
FRESHOUR, Mary ff1812
FRIER, Alexander wwf1788
FRIESE, Michael f1792
FRITZ, Michael wf1772
FROSHOUR, Wendel wf1788; f1792
FRY, Abraham ff1792
  Adam w1861; ff1870; f1874
  Isabella f1844
  Jacob wf1805; f1810
  John f1826
FRYATT, Ann M. w1861
  Bartholemew wf1788
  James f1849; ff1853; f1870; f1873
  Tillotson w1861; f1871
FRYER, Alexander f1792
FULK, Jacob w1812
FULTON, David ff1792
FULTZ, Baltzer f1792
FURGUISON, David f1792
FUSS, Frederick w1854

GAFF, James f1867
GAIN, Sally Jane f1849
GAINOR, Sampson ff1841
GANDY, James f1780
GANO, Daniel ff1825; f1826
  James f1795
  Stephen w1853
GANOE, James f1807
GANTT, John w1849
GARARD, David fff1825; f1826; f1828
  William f1795
GARDNER, Peter w1844; f1867; ff1870
GARRARD, John ff1817
GARRELL, Abraham ff1831; f1840
  William B. fff1841; ff1844
GARRIGAN, David w1808
GARRINGER, Barbara w1808
GATRILL, Richard f1808; ff1817
GEHR, D.G. f1874
  Daniel fff1840; f1841; ff1844;
    f1849

GEHR (Con't.), Elizabeth f1844
    Joseph f1841
    Margaret ff1844
GERRARD, John wf1780; ff1789
    William f1780
GETZENDANER, Charles R. w1853
GIBBONS, Morris ff1795
GILBERT, Nathan wf1780; f1789
GILL, John fff1844
    Sally Jane f1849
    Thomas fff1841
GINGAR, Casper f1789
GLADDEN, Jacob S. ff1878
    William fff1871
GLENN, John wff1780
    James w1774; f1807
    Jane w1789; f1793
    Martha w1774
GODART, John f1774
GOLD, Thomas w1795
    Washington ff1867; ff1871
GORDEN, Thomas f1795
GORRELL, Jacob wf1823; f1844
    Joseph fff1817; ff1823
    Joseph C. f1844
    W.B. f1841
    William w1795; f1807; f1808
GOUDEY, James f1789
GOWAN, Joseph f1808
GRAHAM, James wf1774; f1780
GRANT, Daniel f1780
    Erasmus ff1844
    J. Edward w1789
    Robert f1795
GRANTHAM, David ff1849
    David L. f1871
    Lewis w1875; f1878
    Sarah f1867
    William f1795; f1802; wff1838; f1840;
      f1841; f1844
GRAVES, Sarah f1849
GRAY, David fff1795
    Hugh w1780; f1789
    James W. w1853; ff1871
    Jane w1870
    John f1808; ff1817; ff1825; f1831
    John E. w1831
GREEN, Charles f1787; f1874
    Diannah w1795
    William wff1724; fff1802; wff1841
GREGG, Andrew w1831
GREGORY, Mrs. Mary ff1844
GRIER, James w1853
GRIFFITH, David w1828; f1831
    Elijah fff1871
GRIMM, Mary M. w1874

GRIST, Gravener f1817; f1823; f1825
GROVE, Catherine fff1849
    Michael f1802; f1807
    Peter fff1825; ff1826
    Susan E. w1853; f1871; f1874;
      ff1878
GROWAN (GOWAN), Joseph f1802
GRUBB, Joseph w1831
GUILFORD, John w1774; f1780
GUSTIN, Alpheus f1808
GWILLIAMS, Resin wff1844
GWINN, Daniel f1808

HABERLAND, Louisa f1878
HAGAMAN, Antonette f1832
    John f1832
    Joseph f1825; ff1827
    Marcus f1832
HAINES, Henry w1776; w1786
    Joseph w1829
    Sarah w1829
HAIR, Samuel wff1799
HALDERMAN, J.S. f1874; f1878
HALEY, Reuben w1789
HALL, John f1786
    Joseph wf1796
    Walter f1872
HAMMILL, George A. f1872; f1874
HAMMOND, James ff1805; f1812; f1817
    Otho f1817
    Valentine ff1803
    W.A. f1872
HAMMON, George f1801
    George N. f1868
HANCHER, Nicholas w1776
HANCIWAY, Ann ff1832
HANNA, Jacob Sr. fff1825
    William f1805
HANNER, Jacob w1817
HANNI, Jacob Sr. f1825
HANSELL, Michael wff1779
HARLAM, Silas w1854
HARLAN, Jehu wf1805; ww1844; f1849
    John f1817
    Mary f1796
    Silas ff1848; fff1849
    Stephen w1796; f1805; fff1812
HARLEY, Isabella f1878
    Isabella K. f1878
    Patrick w1861; ff1868
    William f1824; f1878
    William M. f1874; w1876
HARLOW, Elijah f1789
HARMAN, Nicholas wf1805
HARMER, J.H. f1874
HARN, George w1827; ff1829; f1841
    George Sr. ff1827; f1829

(Con't.), Jacob ff1829
Philip C. f1832
Thomas f1829; f1832; f1844
William ff1829
ER, John w1790; ff1794
Robert w1779; f1778; f1805
IS, Benjamin f1802
David f1854
Jacob f1812
Jacob P. f1805
Jacob P. heirs ff1817; f1827
Joseph fff1796
Thomas ff1865
RISON, Dennis W. f1849; w1854
Holland wf1871
Holland W. f1878
James wff1849
John B. fff1839
John S. wf1838; f1848
Dr. John S. Jr. ff1844
Nancy A. f1878
Napoleon B. f1844
Otho H. f1844
Peyton R. w1854
Samuel w1789; w1790
T, Andrew f1794
Thomas w1794; f1796
ISOCK, Joseph f1832
William ff1823; f1829
TZOOK, William f1825
ELET(T), Robert w1817; ff1823
TINGS, Robert ff1817
R, Jacob f1786
ERLEY, Godfrey ff1829
, William f1796
K, Michael f1839
KINS, William ff1796
N, Mary B. f1878
DEN, William H. w1849
MEN, Susan w1854
MER, Susan f1854
S, John wff1786
SLETT, Hester A. f1854
John wfff1849
GES, Barley T. f1865
Benjamin ff1805; f1812
Elijah f1823
Elizabeth w1854
Hezekiah f1844; f1847; f1848;
f1868
James w1803
John f1823
Dr. John f1849
John S. wf1849
Jonas f1803; ff1849
Joshiah M. f1865
Joshua w1789; f1790; w1829; ff1849

Joshua Jr. w1825
Joseph w1817; fff1824
Mary w1796; f1839
Morgan M. wf1854
Oliver J.P. f1868
Oliver P. f1865; f1868
Owen Tuder w1861
Samuel w1817; w1824
Samuel Sr. ff1825
Sarah wf1839
Solomon w1823; f1824; f1825;
ff1827
Susan w1861; f1865; ff1868
HEIN, Jacob w1786
HELAN, Barbara f1817; f1824
HELFERSTAY, Henry wff1849
John ff1844; f1848
Phobe Jo f1849
Susan Virginia f1849
HENDERSON, John f1832
HENDRICKS, James w1796; ff1803
Jehn ff1796
HENERICH, Joshua w1861
HENRY, John f1824
John B. fff1823; f1824; f1827;
f1829; f1832; f1844
Michael w1796; fff1805
Robert ff1796
William w1874
HENSEL, Elizabeth f1874
HENSELL, George ff1868
James H. f1872
James W. f1868
Samuel f1874
HENSHAW, Ann wf1805; ff1824
Harriett B. f1824; w1861; f1872;
f1874
Hiram wff1844
James wffff1865
James D. ff1865
Jonathan f1803; ff1812
Myra A. f1872
Nora f1872
Rhuanne f1812; f1817
William w1805; f1824; f1825
HENTHARN, James W. f1776
HERBERG, Gustave w1861; f1868
HERBERT, Elisha wff1841
HERRING, Amanda M. f1878
Catherine M. f1868
George W. f1868; f1872
Henry M. f1868
HERSHFIELD, Frederick wf1776
HERSHURN, Jacob f1803
HESS, Charles f1779
Charlotte w1849
J.C. f1827

HESSON, Maria f1825
HEYRONEMOUS, Conrad w1829
HIATT, George w1786
HIBBARD, Aaron wf1849
    Egedius wf1849
HIENMALL, Ezecial w1790
HIETT, George f1796
    Simon w1796
HILL, Abraham ff1823; f1839
    Abraham R. f1832
    Ann R.A. f1878
    George f1832; f1839
    Gustavus B. f1878
    Ira E. f1878
    Jacob fff1844
    John A. f1839; f1841; f1844;
      f1848; f1832
    Mary J. f1832
    Mary Jane f1841
    Mary S. f1844
    Melvina f1874
    Rachel ff1832; f1844
    Richard f1839
    Robert f1817
    William f1849; f1854
    William E. f1872; f1878
HITE, Catherine ff1790
    Jacob wff1776; f1796
    John w1776; ff1779
    Mary ff1790
    Sarah ff1790
    Thomas wff1779
HOFFMAN, Abraham w1839
    Catherine f1839
    Frederick ff1825
    Jacob fff1802; f1817
    John fff1805; f1817
    Joseph wf1848; ff1849
    Mary f1817
    Michael fff1805; f1825
    Susanna f1825
    Valentine f1824
HOGDIN, John C. w1861
HOGE, John B. w1825
HOGELAND, Everhart f1779
HOGELIN, John C. f1868
HOKE & SHAW, Peter f1841
HOLLENSBACK, Daniel f1796
HOLLIDA, G.W. ff1861
    George W. f1865
    Harriett L. f1868
    John W. w1867
HOLLIDAY, George f1812
    James wf1802; w1803
    John f1803
    Nancy f1803
    William w1861; f1868; ff1871

HOLLINGER, Charles w1802
HOLLINGSWORTH, D____? f1839
    David w1854
    P. f1839
    Parker f1832
HOLLIS, B.B. f1874
    Thomas P. f1874
HOLMES, Nancy f1854; f1868
HOMER, James H. f1872
HOMRICH, Joshua f1868
HOOKE, Mary w1776
HOOPER, John w1817; fff1825
HOOVER, Mary E. f1868
    Jacob f1796; f1801; f1812
    Martin ff1790
HORGER, Charles w1878
HORICK, George ff1874
HORNER, James W. f1871
HOTT, Ann f1865
HOVERMALE, John wf1812; f1817
HOUCK, Elizabeth f1824; ff1825
    Jacob f1817; f1824; fff1829
    Margaret f1823; f1824; f1839
    Michael wff1817; f1824; f1827;
      w1832
    William f1838
HOUK, Jacob ff1803
    Margaret w1817
HOUKE, Jacob wff1812
    William ff1832
HOUSEMAN, David wf1790; ff1805
    Martin wfff1805
    Elizabeth f1829
HOUSEWORTH, Sarah w1841; ff1844
HOUT, George M. w1844; ffff1848
HOUTE, George wf1786
HOUTS, Emanuel f1874
    Samuel f1878
HOWARD, John w1803
    Robert f1776
HOYLE, Jacob wf1779; f1817
HUBBY, Jay Alder? f1823
HUDGEL, Jehu ff1848
    Resin w1832; f1841; f1844; f1848
    Sarah E. f1849
HUDSON, William w1823; ff1824
HUFFMAN, Catherine ff1832
    Jacob f1812
    John ff1812
    Mary f1812
    Valentine f1812
HUGHES, Isaac f1776; f1779
HULL, George w1779; f1786
    Henry f1790; f1878
HULSE, Josiah f1776; f1790
HUNTER, David wffff1829; f1832; f1839;
    f1841; f1844

10

ER (Con't.), Hugh ff1776
   J.H. f1849
   Moses f1796
   Moses S. f1829
   William w1874
HINSON, Samuel w1861; f1872; f1878

ELLA, John H. ffff1878
AND, George w1844
   Sarah w1878

, Ann f1817
   Ann R. f1805; f1812
   Isaac f1826
   James w1791; f1796; f1805
   Jeremiah fw1779; w1826
   John f1796; f1812
   Nathaniel f1796
   Robert f1825; f1826
   William f1805; f1817
SON, John w1787; f1791
SON, John f1867
EY, Mary Eveline w1873
INS, Asa w1844; f1873
INGS, Edward f1805
   George f1805
, Thomas f1796
T, Samuel fw1812
   William f1791; f1812
SON, Abraham f1817; f1825; f1826
   Hezekiah f1867
   James T. f1867
   Moses f1867
   Robert w1844
   William f1867
STON, Joseph f1826; f1838; f1839
   Moses w1826
   Robert w1826
   William fw1805
S, Elizabeth w1779; w1858; f1867
   James f1799
   John J. f1867
   John Jackson w1844
   Mary f1826
   Peter w1844; f1873; f1867
   Phoebe H. w1844
   Robert fw1796
DAN, Thomas f1796
   William f1823

E, Daniel f1777; f1795
N, Percival w1811; f1817
RNEY, William f1841
RUS, Catherine f1878
TING, Patrick f1874
DY, G. Jacob f1876
S, Philip wff1873; f1874

KEESECKER, Andrew wfff1817; f1829
   Conrad fff1811; f1829
   Elizabeth wf1844
   Henry f1878
   Jacob f1829; f1832; f1841; f1844
   John w1795
   L.A. f1841
   Mary f1829
   Mathias wff1823; f1827
   Samuel f1829
KEEVES, Arthur f1849
KELLER, Andrew f1791
KELLY (KELLEY), Cornelius w1832; f1861
   Thomas wf1805
   William wwff1777
KENDLE, Devault ff1824
KENEASTER, M.A. f1878
KENNEDAY, Daniel f1795; f1805
   Samuel w1817
   Thomas wf1795
KENNEDY, Nancy C. w1849
KEPHART, Bernard ff1829
KERNEY, Elizabeth w1795
   Jacob W.D. f1832
   James B. f1823; f1827; f1829
   James E. ff1832
   John fff1811; ff1832
   John T. w1861
   John W. f1849
   Joseph G. ff1841
   Joshua T. f1849
   Nancy f1849
   Sarah f1791
   William w1787; f1844
KERNS, Catherine w1875
KERS, Peter w1879
KERSNER, Jacob w1795
KERUS, Peter ff1861
KEYS, Frederick f1795
   Gersham f1777
   Humphrey wf1791
   John f1777
   Ruth w1795
KEYSER, John f1811; f1817
KIESSENWITTER, Gotleib w1861
KILMER, Barbara f1855; ff1861
   David ff1841; f1844
   Elie f1841
   Elie D. f1849
   Isaac ff1874; f1876
   John ff1868; f1874
   Polly f1855; ff1861
KING, Matthew f1805
KISER, Joseph ff1844
KISINGER, John wfff1832
KISSINGER, Susan ffff1844
KITCHEN, Amy f1823; f1861; f1868
   Job fff1811; ff1817

KITCHEN(Con't.),Rachel f1817; f1822; f1823
KLECKHAM, Conrad w1777
KLINE, Jacob wf1861
KLINGER, Henry f1805
KNADLER, David f1878
KNIPE, Charles R. wff1876
    Sarah w1861
KNODE, Polly f1841
KNOWSLAR, Conrad w1841
    Randolph w1875
KNOX, William wf1777
KNUP, Valentine wff1823; f1827
KNUPP, Catherine w1829
KOONTZ, Samuel fff1868; f1874
KREGLOW, Adam fff1868
    George wff1823; f1824; f1827;
        f1841; f1845; f1849
    Sarah f1849
KROESEN, Lydia w1855
    Washington ff1878
    William fff1844
KROH, Henry w1823; fff1824; f1827
KRUCK, Jacob w1795
KYER, see MUSETTER
KYLE, Joseph wf1777

LACKEY, James w1774
LADAN, C.W. f1878
    Thomas f1874; wf1875
LADEY, Charles w1803
LAFEVER, Daniel w1877
    Henry ff1825; f1829
    Jacob f1870
LAFEVRE, Hiram f1878
    Maria fff1878
LAISEY, Samuel H. w1861
LAMAR, Martha R. w1876
    William f1862
    William L. f1867
    William Luther f1862
LAMASTER, James f1845
LAMON, George ff1825
    George Sr. w1825; f1827
    John f1809
    Joseph fff1795; ff1804
    Margaret f1838
LANG, James f1849
LANTZ, Christian fff1875
LASHORN, Ralph f1867
LATIMER, Thomas B. ff1845
    Thomas W. f1852
LAUFER, Frederick w1829
LAUGHLAND, Joshua f1774
LAUR, Thomas ff1817
    Thomas Jr. fff1817
LAUVER, Mary w1845
LAVIS, William ff1838

LAYMASTER, Calvin ff1878
    D. f1878
    Daniel f1878
    William f1875
LEACH, Benjamin T. f1875
    Ellen Lee f1875
LEATHERS, William w1874
LEE, Anthony w1832
    Charles wf1774
    John ff1789; f1825
    Mary ff1845
    Samuel wff1838; f1845
    Sarah ffff1845
    Thomas ff1832
LEEBERMAN, Lewis f1867
LEESON, John W. w1804
LEFEVER, Daniel f1829
    David f1829
    Henry w1874; ff1875
    Jacob f1858; w1879
    John f1838
    Margaret ff1829
    Sally f1829
LEAMON, John f1804
LEMASTER, Abraham f1774
    Ann w1861
    Daniel w1862; fff1870; f1878
    John f1849
    John wff1825; f1827; ff1829;
        f1832
    Mary ff1870; f1874
LEMEN, Hiram H. f1875; f1878
    Rhuannah f1804; f1809
LEMON, James wff1774
    John wff1774
    Margaret w1861
    William w1817; f1822; f1825
    Thomas w1832; fff1838; f1841
LEONARD, Nicholas wf1795
LEOPARD, Adam f1825
    Barbara wff1838
    Catherine f1870
    Daniel ff1817; f1822; f1825;
        f1827
    Michael ff1838; ff1841
LEPARD, Adam f1817
LESSLEY, John f1829
LESSLY, John w1825
LETMAN, Valentine wf1795
LEWIS, Catherine w1861
    Christopher f1774
    David f1789
    John f1789
    Margaret w1822
    William f1825
LIGHT, Ann f1829
    Ann W. f1827; f1829

T (Con't.), Elizabeth f1809
  Jacob T. w1861; ff1862; f1867;
    f1870
  Jacob W. wf1832
  John f1832
  John C. w1849
  John Sr. wf1827; f1829
  Rev. John f1878
  Mary Ann w1853; ff1867; ff1870
  Nancy f1832; f1838
  Peter w1804; ff1809; f1825; w1852;
    fff1852; f1854; f1870
  Peter Sr. w1817
  Ruth f1861
JRN, John fff1774
3ORN, Francis wff1774
3AY, Daniel L. f1862
A(E)NFELTER, Abraham ff1804; ff1809;
  ffff1817; f1825
  Elizabeth f1829
  Jacob ffff1878
  N.L. f1875
  Valentine wf1804; f1809; f1817
JN, Susan A. ff1870; f1875
  Susannah w1861
LE, Josiah f1867
LEJOHN, William wf1809
, John f1789
N, James wff1774
, Jacob f1852
  Richard ff1774
E, Meriall f1829
  Merrell f1852
  Mursalla ff1827
  Rosanna w1858
  Thomas wfff1838
HART, Benjamin w1872
, Cookes f1774
  Elizabeth w1861
  Isaac w1861
  James f1852
  John ffff1822; f1829
  Mary wf1829; f1832
  Rebecca f1774
HEIMER, Louis f1875
JN, William w1795
  Richard f1795; f1803
R, Philip wfff1774
RY, James w1809
AN, Richard w1804
Y, John w1861
S, Basil wfff1838; f1845
  Edward wf1774
  Gabriel f1845
  Savisa w1861
, Abigail w1879
R, William w1858

LUTHEY, Jacob f1845
LUTTY, Jacob fff1838
Lyle, Isabella wff1849; f1852
  John ff1795; f1804; f1817
  John R. ff1867; ff1870
  P.O. f1878
  Peggy H. f1822
  Preston O. ff1875
  Robert f1787; f1795; f1804
  Robert W. f1822; f1849
  Sallie D.L. f1875
  William O. f1838; ff1845
LYNCH, Daniel ff1838
LYSLE, Hugh w1789; ff1795; f1820;
  f1822

McABOY, Sarah f1812
  William f1805; f1810; f1812; f1827
McALLISTER, Benjamin f1805; f1822; f1825;
  f1854; f1864; f1868
  C. w1838
  Christ ff1838
  Christopher f1805; f1842; f1843
  Eliza f1827
  Mary f1827
McBRIDE, James f1805
McCARMICK, Charles w1875
McCARTNEY, Benjamin f1772
  John f1812
  Sarah w1780
McCLAREY, Jane w1845
McCLEARY, Jane f1868
  John w1830
  Mary w1877
McCLEMMONS, William f1777
McCLYMONS, William w1772
McCONNELL, James w1871
  William w1805
McCORMACK, John N. f1849
McCOUCH, James ff1843; f1845
  Robert w1805
McCOY, Absolum w1798
  Joseph ff1804
  William fff1822
McDANIEL, Garrel w1854
  Mary w1827
McDEAD, John f1778
McDERMOTT, Cornelius w1858
McDONALD, Andrew w1798
  Bryan w1810
  Charles E. f1878
  George w1864
  James w1865
  John w1865
  Robert ff1854; f1864
  William wf1854

13

McELROY, Ann ff1878
    Patrick f1804; f1805
McGAREY, William w1865
McGARY, William ff1876
McGOVERN, Ann f1837
    Philip f1832
McGOVRAN, Philip w1822
McINTIRE, Henry w1825
    Thomas w1847; fff1845
McKEEVER, Daniel w1830
    Elizabeth fff1864
    John f1805
McKENNEY, Edward w1792
    Mary f1871
    John w1805
McKEVER, Angus wf1837
McKEWAN, Michael ff1798
McKEWEN, Michael w1827
McKIERNAN, Michael f1805
    No Name f1805
McKIERNEY, John f1817
McKINNEY, John f1810
    No Name ff1812
McKINSTRY, Mary S.B. f1876
McKNIGHT, Ann w1812
    Robert wff1805
McKOWEN, Gilbert w1798
McKOWN, Edward f1879
    Gilbert ffff1805
    Isaac f1812; f1819
    Isabella wff1845
    John f1804; w1838; f1842; w1865;
        f1871; f1878
    Laura V. f1865; ff1871
    Maria f1843
    Mary f1871
    Mary Ann w1865; f1879
    Morgan f1838
    Samuel wf1837; f1838; f1843
    Sarah w1854
McKOY, Absolum f1817
McMANNUS, Hugh f1861
McPHERSON, Daniel wf1788
McQUILKEN, Jacob ff1845; f1847
McSHERRY, Bernard f1796; f1798
    Cecilia Helen w1854
    James H. f1871
    Richard w1865; f1871
    Susan A. w1865
MACCUBBIEN, George W. wff1879
MACKEY, James William f1805
    Moses f1838; ff1842; f1843; f1845
    Ruth wf1832
    William wf1812
MAGAW, John wff1812
MAHONEY, Ann w1865

MALLONRY, William f1858
MALLORY, George F.B. w1854
MANFORD, John f1864; f1871
MANOR, Samuel ff1847
MANSFIELD, Stephen f1854
MARCHANT, Isaac fff1819
MARLOTT, Abraham ff1805; ff1830
    Elizabeth f1832
MARQUART, Nicholas fff1838
MARSHALL, James ff1805
    John f1819; ff1822
MARTIN, Banajah? f1786
    George ff1827
    James w1865; f1864
    Zeptha w1822; ff1825; f1827
MASLIN, William wff1854; f1864; f1868
MASON, Alexander fff1830
    James w1812
    Rachel f1812
    William ff1830; f1832
MATHEWS, Enoch f1832; f1837
    John wfff1777
    William f1777
MAURER, Stephen w1832
MAXWELL, James w1849
    Jane w1865
MAY, Daniel w1777; ff1780
    James w1861; f1864
MAYBERRY, Rebecca w1864
MAYBURRY, Sarah Ann w1865
MAYERS, Jane fff1871
MAYHEW, William w1842; fff1845; f1847
MEAD, S.B. f1878
MEANOR, Samuel f1847
MEANS, George A. f1876
    William H. f1876
MEDLEY, William w1792
MELICK, Philip w1796; f1798
MELLENBURG, August w1849
MENDENHALL, James fff1819; f1827
    John wf1772
MENGHINI, Joseph fff1827; f1830
    Overton w1830
MENSER, George w1838; fff1842
MERCER, Edward wf1783; ff1798; f1805
MERCHANT, Isaac w1812; f1845
    Nancy ff1841 f1843
    William wf1772; wff1830
MERRIOT, Barbara wf1777; f1780
    George wf1772
MERRITT, Barbara f1792
METZ, Catherine f1871
MICHAEL, Michael ff1792
MIDDLETON, Adam f1788
    Thomas wf1812; f1812
MILES, Loyd wfff1812

S(Con't.), Ruth wfff1812
AN, John w1786
    Robert f1787
ENBURG, August fff1868
ER, A.C. f1871
    Aaron f1871
    Abraham f1847
    Absolum f1805; f1827
    Agnes w1805
    Barbara ff1832
    Barbary w1832
    Charles w1805
    Christina w1819
    D.D. f1841; f1842
    Daniel ff1798
    David wf1780; ff1827; ff1829; fff1830;
        f1841; f1842; ff1849; f1876
    David E. f1847
    David H. f1832; ff1871
    Elizabeth f1838
    Ellen f1843
    Elon wf1819; ff1822; ff1825; f1827
    George f1825; f1832; f1837
    Hannah f1788; f1871
    Henry w1805; wf1817; ffff1822; w1842;
        ff1843
    Hester ff1825
    Hugh wf1792
    J.P. f1876
    Jacob ff1798; f1805; f1830
    Jacob H. w1854
    Jacob L. f1871
    James f1792; f1796; f1819; f1825;
        f1832; wff1837
    John wf1788; fff1798; fff1805; ww1832;
        f1854
    John C. f1858; w1865
    John L. f1867
    Joseph f1812; wf1819; f1822; ff1825
    Joseph S. w1850
    Madison f1841
    Mary f1812; ff1832; w1849; f1876
    Mary Ann f1832; f1843
    Mary R. f1876
    Michael ff1805; f1817; f1876
    Michael L. w1865
    Norman f1867
    Phillip w1796; ff1798
    Robert f1788
    (in Wis?) Robert Carter wf1778
    Sallie f1871
    Sarah Jane f1847
    Uriah f1812; f1819; f1822
    William D. w1822; f1825; fff1827; f1829
    William H. ff1849
    William M. f1871

    William S. f1842
    William f1812; f1819; f1832
    Zachariah w1792; f1796; w1812; ff1817
MINGHINI, Joseph w1832; f1849
MITCHELL, William H. ff1864
MIXWELL, Adam ff1832; f1838
MOALER, George Adam f1792
MOLER, Adam wf1783; f1796
    Henry wf1798; ff1810
MONG, George ff1832
    John fff1843; ff1849
    Mary ff1849
    William H. w1876; f1876; f1878
MONK, Owen R. f1792
MONTAGUE, Christopher w1865; w1874
MORGAN, Elizabeth ff1837; f1838
    Elizabeth Ann ff1827
    George ff1810
    Isaac w1783
    J.B. f1849
    J.P. f1849
    Jacob wff1780
    Jeptha ff1845; f1847
    Josiah H. ff1827; f1830; w1865;
        f1871; ff1876
    Levi ff1827; f1830; ff1837; f1838
    Lucinda f1827; f1832; ff1838; f1868
    Mary ff1819; w1830
    Morgan wf1796; f1798; f1825; f1827;
        f1832
    Olivia w1843; f1849; f1854
    Prisilla w1819; ff1822
    Rawleigh f1830; fff1825
    Samuel f1827; w1822
    Thomas f1864
    William wf1788; w1792; f1796; f1798
    Zachariah f1805; f1810
MOON, Simon ff1822
MOONEY, Joseph f1805; f1812
MOORE, Archibald f1805
    Cato w1796; ff1804
    David w1871
    (Moon),Deborah wf1837
    Isaac E. ff1878
    Jacob w1804; fff1805
    James wff1864
    John wf1783
    Joseph wf1780
MORLEY, A. ff1848
MORRISON, Abigail w1832
    Bessie f1876
    Brownie ff1878
    Daniel B. f1837; w1861; f1864;
        ff1867; f1868; ff1871
    Hannah ff1825; f1827
    Jesse w1847; ff1849
    Nathan w1805
    Richard ff1827; ff1830

MORRISON (Con't.), William f1780; w1832;
    ff1837; f1838
    William B. f1838; f1849; f1845;
      f1854; f1864
MORRIS(S), Elizabeth wf1792
    Richard A. f1822; f1827; f1832
MORROW, Charles w1792; ff1792
    J.R. heirs ff1878
    Jane L. fff1871
    Joseph R. ff1868; ff1871
MUHLENBERG, W. & N. f1871
MULLINS, Nathaniel f1796
MUMMA, Jacob w1847
MURLEY, Arandle f1845 (Crandle?)
MURPHEY, Philip P. f1845; f1847
    William f1780; ff1783
MURPHY, John wwf1798; f1805
    John V. w1876
    Joseph ff1878
    Michael w1876
    William fff1838; f1847
MURRAY, Zachariah f1827
MURRY, Zachariah wf1819; f1822
MUSETTER and KYER f1849
MYERS, Aaron w1865; fff1871
    Anna Mary w1865; f1864
    Barbara E. ff1864
    Barbary E. w1861
    C. Groves f1827
    Catherine f1832; ff1842; w1876
    Cromwell L. fff1864
    David w1878
    Effie E. f1854
    Effa f1871
    Henry ff1838; wff1854; f1864; fff1868
    Jacob fw1854; f1864
    John wfff1832; f1842; f1849; wfff1878
    John H. fff1838
    Martin w1819
    Mary ff1838; f1842; w1871
    Mary Ann ff1868; f1871
    Peter f1838
    Teter ff1866; w1865
MYLES, George ff1772
    Richard f1805

NACE, Henry w1794; f1810
NADENBOUSCH, James f1845
    Mary f1824
    Mary Ann⁻ w1830
    Philip w1861
NARRINGTON, Ann R. f1867
    John W. f1867
    Joshua ff1849
    Mary H. f1867
NEAD, Daniel Sr.w1823
NEFF, Ezekiah w1861; ff1867; f1872
NEWBAUGH, Ann w1849
    William w1845

NEWCOMER, Alexander f1867
NEWKIRK, George w1823; fff1824
    James wfff1817; ff1823
NEWLAND, John w1794
    William wf1794
NEWSON, Alexander ff1826
NICHOLAS, Amos wff1817; f1823
    John f1824
    Mathias f1804; ff1810
NICHOLS, Ann E. f1845
    Ann Elizabeth f1830
    Eliza f1828
    John f1824; fff1828
    Theresa w1826
NICHOLSON, A.L. w1867
    Thomas w1879
NIPE, Charles f1877
    George wff1838; f1844; f1854; f1867
    Ida May f1877
    John ff1867
    Mary w1854; f1861; f1867
NOLAND, Mary ff1872; w1876; fff1877
    Obed fff1830
    William f1804
NOLL, Ann Maria w1849
    Gatlip w1876
    George wfff1830; ff1838
    Henry ff1845
NORMAN, David w1810
NORTH, Eliza w1854
NOURSE, James f1785; f1804
NUTT, Thomas f1849

OBANION, Bryan f1789
    Bryant wf1779
    John f1795
ODEN, Alexander P. wfff1832; f1838
    Archibald ff1847
    Elias f1832
O'DRISKELL, No Name f1852
OLER, George Adam f1789
OLIVER, John wf1886
OLLEBAUGH, John f1838
OLLER, Peter wffff1823
    Frederick f1789; f1805
ORR, James w1852
    John H. f1832
    William fff1837
ORRICK, Ann f1838
    Charles wf1832
    Mary ff1825
    Nicholas wf1779; f1786
    Susannah f1779
    William w1795; f1805; ff1823
OSBURN, James wf1779
OSBORN, Joseph fff1825
OTT, Nicholas ff1795
OULERBAUGH, Jacob ff1795; f1809
OWEN, Thomas f1795
OZBURN, Davies w1779
    Jonathan w1779

16

See page 26 for
PAGE,PAINSEL,PAINTER,P.

AKER, Hannah f1827
AY (PEREGARY), Joel ff1878
R, Richard w1827
  John wf1775
, John fff1841
, James f1785; f1795; ff1879
3amuel w1795
N, Rosanna f1795
RSON, George W. wf1874
William wf1775; ff1785
N, William fff1825
RFF, Andrew f1827
  Andrew f1827; f1829
Hugh fff1827
, John wf1775
William wff1775; f1825
, George wf1795; f1808
Hannah w1861; ff1874
Jesse w1861; ff1864; f1867; f1874
John C. w1861; f1867
Martin w1817; fff1823; ff1827
Nathan D. w1861
3arah w1861; f1867; f1872
William f1827; ff1829
E, _ean w1795; f1805
, John ff1832
ETON, Elizabeth A. w1861
Mary w1861
Nathaniel w1785
P.C. f1867; f1874; f1879
Philip w1795; f1823
Philip C. ff1864; fff1867; ff1872
3arah w1861
William wff1817; f1825
Y, John D. f1878
John D.R. ff1878
R, Joshua f1805
ARY (PAREGAY), Joel f1874
LL, Alineda f1844
L, John f1832; f1838
, Robert f1874
3amuel w1795
PS, Charles wf1785
Thomas f1775
PS, Ruth f1832; f1838
Resin f1849
NG, John T. f1874
  J.W. f1874
John W. f1874; f1879
NOGLE, Samuel f1872
R, Catherine f1827
Eliza A. f1878
Elizabeth w1825
George f1827
Hannah ff1872; f1874
John fff1827; fff1867

Joseph f1827
Margaret f1827
Martin w1861; fff1867; f1872; f1874;
  f1878; f1879
Mathias wf1812; f1827
Michael wf1817
Rachel f1827
PLOTNER, Daniel wff1838; f1841; f1844
  John ff1785; f1795
Morris w1808
PLUMMER, Joseph wf1805; f1808; f1827
POINTS, Mary E. f1844
POISAL, C.W. f1849
  John f1864
Peter w1808
POISALL, Jacob ff1838
POLAND, Samuel ff1775
POLLOCK, Allen wf1795
PORTER, John W. w1844; f1849
PORTERFIELD, A. f1838
  A.W. ff1864; fff1867; f1874
Alexander wf1795
Anna May f1879
Archibald f1829; ff1832; f1841
Charles w1825; f1832
Elizabeth fff1817
George f1825; f1854
George Jr. ff1827; f1829; fff1841;
  ff1844
Hannah w1849
John wff1825; fff1827; f1829
Mary f1864
Mary A. f1874
Mary E. f1872; w1874
Mathew w1795
Nancy w1817
Rachel f1849
William wf1817; ff1823
William L. f1879
POTTERHOFF, Andrew w1825
POTTEROFF, Andrew f1829
POTTINGER, Robert f1775
POTTS, John wf1808
POWELL, A.M. f1841
  Archibald M. ff1844
Mary P. w1861
Rebecca f1844
Robert fff1823
Thomas wff1849
W.W. f1878
W.W.T. f1874
PRICE, Daniel wf1854; f1861
Ignatius f1785; ff1795
Jacob wff1808; f1812
James f1872

PULSE, Jacob f1795
    Michael f1805
    Mary w1854; f1864
PULTZ, Mary E. f1864
    Michael ff1805
PYKE, Michael wf1775
    William wf1775
PYLE, Mefflin w1864
    Richard ff1775

QUADE, Charity Ann f1825
QUIGLEY, Elizabeth f1817; f1825
    John f1806; f1817
QUINN, James ff1804; ff1806

RACOB, Jacob wf1796
RAINEFELDT, John M. ff1811
RAMER, Catherine B. f1844
RAMSBERGER, Henry f1824; ff1827
    Mary f1824
RAMSBURG, Henry ff1806; ff1817
    Elizabeth w1861; ffff1872
RAMSEY, Samuel wff1806; f1817
RANDALL, Robert f1817
RANDELS, Roger f1811
RANDOLPH, James f1788
    John wff1788
RANK, Valentine f1863
RANKIN, Benjamin w1774
RAY, Samuel Sr. f1824
REAGAN, Burket w1774
REDMAN, Robert f1788
REED, Exer fff1878
REEL, Daniel f1827
    Elizabeth w1817; fff1822
    Peter ff1817; f1822
    Sarah f1829
REES, Ellis w1844
    Enoch w1796
    Jacob f1811; w1824; f1827
    Margaret f1848
    Thomas w1817; f1822; f1827;
      f1832
REIFF, Charles wf1861; f1873
    William Henry f1854
REIS, Philip ff1878
RENTCH, L.S. f1874; f1878
    L.T. ff1874
REYNOLDS, George f1868; f1872; ff1878
RHINEFELT, John w1811
RHODES, John f1796; f1802
RICE, James Sr. w1863
RICHARDS, Henry B. ff1878
    Lucy w1824; f1827
    Thomas ff1878
RICHARDSON, George S. f1874
    G.W. f1878

George W. f1874; f1878
    John w1806
    Joseph f1788
RIDENOUR, John w1806; f1811
RIDGEWAY, John f1788
RIDING, E.H. ff1874
RILEY, Elizabeth w1861; f1872
    John f1774; wf1788; f1796
    John T. f1872; f1874; f1878
    Richard f1802
    S.J. f1878
    Sarah Jane fff1878
RINGER, Catherine ff1868
RINER, Henry ff1832; ff1878
    Jacob w1854
    Laura M. f1878
RIPLEY, Joseph w1774
RIPLEY (RIPPEY?), Matthew w1817
RIPPY, Matthew w1837; ff1838; f1841;
    f1844
RIPPEY, Rebecca w1844; ff1848
ROACH, Ann f1806
    James fff1806
    William ff1874; f1878
ROBENS, Job f1837
ROBBINS, C.K. ffff1878
    Conrad w1861
    Elvina ff1848
    George f1848
    J.K. f1848
ROBERTS, Boyd wff1848
    Hannah fff1811
    John w1861
    Jonathan fff1806
    Mary ff1878
    Mary B. f1878
    Samuel wff1796; wf1832; f1837;
      f1838
ROBINS, Catherine fff1841
    John K. w1848
ROBINSON, Alexander ff1806; f1811; w1861;
      f1874
    Angelia w1848
    George w1817; ff1822; f1824
    George W. f1863; f1868; f1873
    Israel w1827; ff1829; ff1832;
      f1841; f1873
    James f1796; wf1806; f1811; w1832;
      f1837; f1838; f1841
    James H. ff1872; wf1873; f1874;
      f1878
    James Jr. f1854
    James (of Israel) f1837
    James R. fff1844; f1848
    Jane w1844; f1846; fff1848
    John S. f1874

NSON (Con't.), Joshua fff1827
Lucy M. f1874
Martha J. f1878
Mary E. ff1863
Newton f1872
R.K. f1878
Robert K. ff1878
Samuel f1837; wff1848
Thomas wf1837; fff1838
ESTER, Elizabeth f1802
ER, Ernest f1872; f1874
INS, Martha fff1878
N, Thomas wl811
Y, Michael ff1863
, John wf1788
EY, Michael wff1837; f1838
, Daniel ff1874
Jacob f1838; ffff1878
Mary ff1838; f1841
Solomon ff1832; f1837; f1838;
    fff1841; ff1844
, Jonathan wf1774
NBERGER, Anthony wff1848; f1868
Nancy f1848; f1854
, Conrad f1796
, Ann wf1841
Conrad wl788
Stephen wf1774; f1788
CH, Conrad w1861
Andrew fff1824; ff1827; f1829;
    f1844
George ff1838
Nicholas ff1817; ff1822
H, Nicholas Jr. f1824; ff1829
AND, William J. f1872
Lewis f1788
Renoes f1774
(RAY?), Samuel ff1817
EY, James wf1788; f1796
, Valentine f1868
ER, William ff1832
, Abraham fff1811; f1817
Jacob f1806; f1822; f1848
Leonard wl774
Sallie f1878
Sarah ffff1827; f1837
William wl817; ff1822; f1841
William Jr. f1817
ELL, James f1796; f1841
James B. ff1837
Rebecca wff1774
LER, Elizabeth fff1878
John L. ff1878
ERFORD, Elizabeth f1878
Robert f1774; f1788
Thomas wl848
, Joseph wl774
AL, George f1878

RYNON, John wf1774; f1788

SEIBERT, William T. ff1849
SELLERS, Martin fff1836; w1829
Samuel ff1868
SENAKER, John B. f1866
SENKER, John B. wl854
SENSENDIVER, Jacob f1878
Lewis f1875; ff1868
SEWELL, John wf1793; f1795; f1798
SHAFFER, George wf1860
Henry wl849
John wl877; ff1875
L.M. f1875
Margaret f1871
Peter ff1817; f1818
SHARP, John f1800
Thomas wl808; f1812
SHARPE, Thomas f1800; f1818
SHARTLE, Jacob f1818
SHAVER, Michael f1783; f1789
SHAW, Frederick f1812
Theodore fff1808
SHEAR, Henry f1808
SHEARER, Archibald wf1800
Henry ff1805
John fff1774
Rachel f1824
Rachell ff1823
Sarah wff1805
Thomas ff1812; f1824
SHEETZ, Philip wl793; wf1800; wff1849
SHELTON, Joseph L. f1860
SHENTON, Joseph L. f1868
Mary L. f1849; wl849
SHEPHERD, Abraham wf1849
Elizabeth wl789
Thomas wfff1774; wl789; ff1805; f1812
SHERRARD, John f1849
Joseph f1825; f1829
SHEWALTER, Elizabeth wf1838
Joseph f1838
SHIELDS, John f1808
Mary wl824
Sarah wl829; f1836
William wl829
SHIMP, John wff1836; f1838
SHOAFSTALL, George fff1818
John ff1800; f1818
SHOCKEY, Jacob wl817; ff1818
SHOFSTALL, George wl817
SHOOK, John ff1836
SHOWALTER, Caroline f1838
Elizabeth ff1842
Joseph ff1827; ff1829; f1838
William A. f1845
SHOWARS, Ezekiel f1866; fff1868; ff1871;
    f1873; f1874; f1875; wwl862

19

SHOWARS (Con't.), Susan ffl868; fl873
SHOWERS, Ezekiel fffl878
SHRYOCK, Henry fl798
    Leonard fl774; fl798
SHUART, George fl868
    Mary E. fl875; fl878
    Mary S. fl878
SIGLER, Jacob fl854
    John ffl842
SILBORN, Francis wl774
SILER, Andrew fl800; fl812
    Ben fl842
    Bennett fl873; fl875
    Henry fwl874; fl875
    Jacob wfl800; ffl875
    John ffl848
    Lucy T. fl878; fl879
    Margaret fl818; fl823
    Peter fl805
    Philip ffl838; fl841
    Sarah J. fl878
    Sarah Jane fl879
SILVER, Margaret fl824
    Mary wl825; fl829
SIMMONS, James D. fl864
SIMPSON, William fl800
SKELDING, John fl788
SKINNER, William wfl793
SLAGLE, George C. fl824
    Jacob fl827
    Maria fl825
SLATTERY, Patrick wl862
SLAUGHTER, Amelia wl818; fl823
    Francis wl838
    George fl848
    Mary wl842
SLIGH, Frederick wfl800
SLOAN, James fl841
SLOCUM, Isaac ffl793
SLONAKER, Michael fl875; wl877
SLYER, Charles M. fl873
    Samuel wl862
SLYH, Frederick fl808
SMALL, George fl827 /others
    Adam fl774
    Alice R. fl875; fl878
    Frank P. fl874
    George fffl825
    Henry fffl827
    Jacob wl829; fl836; fl848
    Jacob A. wl862; ffl868; fl873; fl874;
      fl878
    Mary C. ffl875
    William fffl842; fl849; fl868; fl878
    William H. fl875
SMITH, Alexander fl800
    Casper fffl825
    Jacob ffl827; fl829; fl860; wl862;
      ffl873; fl875

    Jacob E. fl860
    Jeremiah wl876
    Jesse ffwl827; fl829
    John wl798; wfl800; fl812; wfl873
    Jonas ffwl879
    John W. fl866; ffl868
SAKEMAN, Anthony fffl845
SANKS, Nancy wl845
SAUNDERS, James ffl849
SAVELEY, Catherine fffl812
SAVERLY, Frederick fl805; fl808
SCHILKAMP, Theodore wl879
SCHOEFIELD, Catherine wl850
SCHOPPART, Adam wl855
    Jacob ffl874; fl875; wl862
    Nichalas wl824; fl825; fl827
    Philip ffl825; wl818
SCHRODE, John fffl818
    Solomon wl818; fffl824
SCOTT, George wfl788
    John George fl808
SEABURN, George wfl795
SEAMAN, Jacomiah (Jeremiah?) ffl783
    Jonah wfl783; fl795
    Jonathan wl783
    Phoebe wl805
SEARS, Oscar A. wl862
SEARY, Thomas wl862
SECHMAN, Barbara wfl829; ffl836
    Benjamin ffl823; fl825
SECKMAN, Catherine fffl845
SEEVER, Peter wl774; fl783; fl789
SEIBERT, Barnett C. fffl875; fl878
    C.C. fl878
    Catherine fl825; fl875; wl877;fffffl
    Catherine M. fl875
    Frederick wfl812
    Eliza wl875
    Elizabeth wl875
    George fffwl878
    George B. ffl829; fl829
    George D. fl866; ffl868
    Harrison S. fffl866
    Henry fl800
    Henry J. wfl860; ffffl873
    Jacob wl829; fffl836; fl838;
      fl849; wl855; fl864; fl868;
      fl873; fl878
    John wl818; ffl823; fl824; fl827; fl
    John N. ffl864
    John S. wl829
    Luther T. fl868
    Maria fl848
    Mary A. fffl873
    Mary E. fl868
    Michael ffl848; wl858; fl860
    Michael K. wl862; fl868

RT (Con't.), Otho W. fff1864
Sarah A. w1878
Sarah J. f1878
Sophia f1873
Susan L. f1868; f1873
Wendell w1800; fw1805
William L. ffff1849; f1873
I, Lucinda w1862
Mary Ann f1845
Nicholas w1862
T.C. w1842
Thomas w1789
Thomas C. fff1842; f1845
William f1783
William T. ff1878
C, Edward wf1798
TE, Edward f1805
P, Jacob H. ff1873
ER, Abraham w1845; fff1845
Hannah f1827
Henry ff1812
Jacob f1795; wf1789
ELY, David f1807; f1808
John ff1808; f1817
GRASS, Ann wff1849
Ann E. f1854
Catherine w1829
Catherine S. fff1845
Elizabeth f1854
John wff1783
R.V. ff1866; f1868
Robert wf1829; f1849
Robert Jr. fff1825
Robert Sr. ff1836
Robert V. wff1860; f1864; f1868
Sallie fff1875
Stephen f1836
Stephen R. wff1849
William f1817; fff1836; f1842; f1848
William Jr. f1868
William T. w1871; f1875
, George f1774
Guy f1793
DEAL, George ff1836
Peter fff1827; f1829
ER, Balser w1812
Catherine w1849
Charles w1864; f1874; f1878
George ff1841; f1842
Henry wfff1805; f1808
Ironi f1873
Jacob f1805
John w1812
John O. w1877
ER, Cather w1859
R, Randolph f1800
Mary f1800

SOISTER, Daniel f1829
SOPER, Catherine f1860
Frederick f1812; ff1808
SOUDER, John f1808
Rudolph f1783
SOUDERS, John f1789
SOUTHER, John f1783
SOUTHWOOD, Edward w1824; f1864
Edward C. f1865
Rhuhannah f1875; w1862
SPECK, B.C. f1879
Benjamin C. w1879
Melissa f1848
Peter w1829; f1842; f1860
SPERO, George f1838; ff1845
Rebecca f1842
SPEROW, Elizabeth f1868
George ff1829
Sarah fff1838; f1841
SPITZNOGLE, John f1838
Mary w1854
Samuel f1845; w1862
SPRIGG, Robert w1849
SPRINKLE, Clinton H. f1864
Damarius T. f1864; f1868
Jacob M. f1864
Manilla f1864
Marrietta C. f1874; f1871; f1864
Welcome E. w1859
Zackery C. f1866
Zach T. f1864
SPROWL, Samuel f1783; f1800
STALEY, Jacob fw1793
STANLEY, Archibald fff1849
Isaac f1793; f1800
John f1849; wff1845
Joseph E. ff1874
Robert f1875
STARRY, Conrad f1836
STARTZMAN, Jacob f1873
John ff1874; ff1875
STEEL, John f1825
STEIFEL, Julius f1875
STELLERMIER, Casper w1818
STELLINGER, Casper ff1824; f1825
STEPHEN, Adam w1789
John w1848
Robert w1808; f1812
STEPHENS, Benjamin w1860
Julia M. w1862
STEPHENSON, Hugh w1774
James w1800
Richard wfffff1774; f1783; f1789;
f1798; wf1793; f1795
STERN, Robert B. wff1818; ff1824
STEVENS, Thomas H. ff1841
STEWART, A. w1854

21

STEWART (Con't.), Charles D. w1854
    Harriet f1849
    George wff1789; f1793
    John w1798
    John W. w1876; ff1875
    Robert f1873; f1875
    Robert E. f1868; f1873
    Robert H. w1879
    Robert Sr. ff1860; w1862
STICKWELL, Bazil w1818
STILWELL, James w1812
STIP, Frances ff1848
    Frederick wf1808
    Peter f1774
STIPP, J. f1868
    Jacob fff1866
    Josiah ff1873; f1874
    Martin w1795; f1800
    Mary ff1873; ff1875; f1879
STOCKTON, Robert f1774
STOKE, Anderson f1808
STOOKEY, Jacob wff1842
    John f1848
    Margaret f1848
    Michael f1848
    Sarah f1848
STOUT, Philip f1818
STOUTS, Philip w1817
STRAYER, Adam Jr. w1818
    Jacob fff1827
    Michael f1812
    Nicholas Jr. f1805
    Nicholas w1808; f1812
STRIBLING, C.K. f1879
STRICKLEY, Conrad f1800
STRIDER, Kelian wf1808
    Philip f1805
STRIDLEY, Frederick w1829
STRODE, Amos f1808
    Eleanor P. fff1873
    James wf1793; fff1808; f1812;
        fff1825; f1827
    Jeremiah w1783; f1798
    John ff1800; fff1808
    Joseph f1817; fff1873
    Priscilla f1817; f1818
    Samuel Jeremiah f1795
    William f1800
STROOP, Elizabeth w1774
    Henry wf1783
STROPE, Melehon f1774
STRUPE, Henry f1789
STRYDER, Isaac w1793
STUART, George ff1864
STUBBLEFIELD, James w1849
STUCKEY, Barbary ff1875; w1876; f1878
    C.W. f1875; f1878

    Charles W. f1873
    David f1868; f1873; f1875; ff1878
    Jacob fff1845; f1868; f1874; f1875
    Jacob Jr. f1868
    John fff1838; f1842
    Susan f1875
    Susanna ff1878
SUBER, Elizabeth f1829
    Mary f1829
    Rebecca ff1825; f1827
SUMMER(S), Lydia R. f1874
    Martha J. f1849
    Martha Jane f1847
    Reuben f1868; w1862
SUTTER, John Sr. f1860
SUVER, Susanna wf1849
SWANEY, John f1817
SWARTZ, C.J. f1875
    Mathias wf1842
    Thomas H. f1866
SWEARINGEN, H.H. w1838; f1842; f1845
    Sarah w1799
    Thomas w1774; f1783; w1808; f1788;
        ffw1812; f1817
    Van w1783; f1788; f1789; wf1789
SWEENEY, Mary w1845
SWERINGEN, Josiah f1800
SWIFT, Godwin w1795; f1812
    Martha wff1825; f1827
SWIGAR, Jacob fffw1774
SWINGLE, Benjamin f1860; f1848
    Benoni f1860
    Eve f1868; f1849
SWIMLEY, George ff1827
    Henry f1829
    Jacob wff1823; f1825; f1838
    Jefferson f1829; f1827; f1842
    John w1862
    Joseph f1827; f1829; f1838
    Martin f1827; f1829
SYESTER, Daniel w1827; ff1829
SYLER, John ff1812; f1842; f1817

TABB, Ann w1848; f1878
    Edward T. fff1867
    Elizabeth wf1818
    George wff1829; w1832; w1854; f1874
    Harriet f1836
    John wff1841
    Milared f1836
    Robert wf1775
    Robert E. wf1867
    S.E. ff1878
    Seaton E. f1878
    Thomas ff1829
TABLER, Adam wff1836; f1838
    Charles w1848; w1861; fff1867; f1874
        f1878

ER (Con't.), Charles (of A.) ff1864; f1867
  Elizabeth w1874
  George wff1826; f1829; f1836
  George W. f1878
  Harrison f1841
  Henry ff1836
  Julia Ann w1848
  Levi ff1878
  Philip H. f1848
  Phoebe fff1838
  William w1841; f1848; ff1864
  William M. w1848
EW, William W. ff1848
·, David James w1836
  Elizabeth ff1838; ff1841; w1843
  Hannah ff1867
  Hannah J. w1861
  John wff1818; w1837
  John Sr. f1824
  Magnus ff1824; ff1826; f1829
  Mary w1841; ff1848
  Rachel w1861
·OR, Isaac f1775
  John w1786; f1796
  Samuel w1783; fff1786; ff1867
·OROY, Andrew w1775
·P, Nathaniel wff1824
·CHER, Hannah fff1848
  Jonathan w1841; ff1841; f1848
  Samuel wff1775
  Stephen ffff1803
·FORD, Jacob w1783
·AS, A.J. f1878
  George f1796
·BURG, Isaac N. f1841
  Morgan K. f1841
  Sarah w1786
·PSON, Cornelius fff1812; f1818; f1838
  David ff1878
  Elisha f1822
  John fw1818
·NBURG, Benjamin f1786; f1796
  Isaac w1848
  John ff1775
  Thomas f1803; f1864
  Thomas Sr. f1810; wf1786
·CKMORTON, Job wff1775; f1822; f1826
  John w1848; f1874; w1775; f1786
  Robert wff1796; f1822
  William f1796
·NEY, Jacob w1783
·STON, John f1775; f1810
  William f1775
·EY, George f1786; f1796
·ERLAKE, William w1878
·LE, George wf1775
·S (TITUS), Francis w1810; f1812

TOOLE, James ff1803; f1818
TOUP, George w1879
TROPNELL, Joseph f1867
TRAVERS, John Meade w1775
TROUTMAN, Mary Ann f1841
TULLEY, Moses f1775
TULLIS, Moses w1775
TURNER, Carlyle f1848
  Ehud f1848; f1854; f1812
  Isabella f1812
  Jesse fff1841
  John ff1786; wf1810; f1812; f1829
  Lydia f1812
  Magill f1848
  Mary w1775; f1783; f1826
  Rachel f1812
  Ruth wf1812; f1829
  Simon fff1826
  Thomas f1848

UNGER, Catherine ff1865; f1867
  Joseph ffw1865
  Nicholas w1813; w1817

VAIL, Edward f1837
  Winfield f1822
VANARSDALER, Cornelia f1776
VANCE, Hugh fw1786
  Joseph fw1796; f1804
  Rachel w1809
VAN METER (METRE), Abraham w1776; f1796
  Abraham Sr. fw1831; f1837
  Abraham E. f1878
  Abraham P. w1837; f1864
  Asahel w1861; f1864
  Henry fw1786
  Isaac fw1826; f1829; f1836
  Isaac Jr. w1831
  Isabella f1818
  Jacob f1809
  John fw1804; w1818; f1824; f1826
  Mollie f1878
  Mollie S. f1871
  Mary f1878
  Nathan f1818; f1822; f1824; f1826
  Philip f1871
  Philip C. w1861; f1864; f1871; f1874
  Thomas w1864; f1871; f1874; f1878
  Van f1861; f1871; f1874; f1878
VARNER, Paul fw1809; f1822
VEAL, Isaac f1804
VEDIER, James w1776; f1786
VEST, Daniel f1786
VESTALL, John f1776
VINCENT, Sarah f1864; f1874; f1878

VINSON(CEN)HELLER, George f1829; f1831
        Henry f1829; f1831
        Jacob f1829; f1831; w1837; f1864
        John w1824; f1829; f1831
        Mary f1829; f1831
        Philip f1796; f1809; f1831; f1837
VIOLET, Leroy f1786; f1796
        Thomas w1809; f1818

WAGER, Gerard B. w1848
WAGGONER, Andrew ff1812; f1822; f1817; f1831
        Christopher w1788
WALKER, Elias M. f1874
        James f1825; ff1827
        William N. f1866
WALLS, George ff1778; w1788
        Mary f1827
WAITE, Harrison ff1846
WALTERS, Ann E. f1866
        Catherine w1852; f1866
        George W. f1878
        Harrison W. ff1873; f1866
        John ff1842; f1846
        John P. w1863; fff1873
        Michael w1841; f1852
        Nancy ff1873
        Sarah C. f1878
WALTON, Michael f1852
WANDLING, Alexander f1852
        George S. f1873
        Jonathan fff1842
WARD, Alexander f1827
        Aquilla f1804; f1812; f1827
        Eliza Jane f1866
        Elizabeth w1861
        Jacob f1832; f1846
        James ff1817
        Joel wf1832; ff1838; f1873; f1874
        Jospeh w1778; f1778; fff1839; f1841
        Joshua fff1788; fff1873
        Mary f1827
        William ff1832; f1838
WARM, Michael fff1788
WASHINGTON, Charles w1795
        Ferdinand f1788
        Samuel w1778
        Susanna wf1778
        Thomas ff1788
        Thornton wf1778; ff1788
WATSON, John fff1778; f1832; f1839; f1842;
        f1843
        John Sr. w1778
        Sarah w1839
        Thomas wf1788; f1791; w1873
WATTS, James f1852
        Nancy w1873
        Nancy W. ff1866
WAYMAN, Thomas w1832

WEAGER, William f1874
WEANING, John A. w1863
WEAVER, Christopher w1778
        George S. f1866
        Helena S. w1863
        Jacob w1843; ff1866
        John ff1822; f1825
        Joseph f1831
        Mary ff1866
WEDDLE, John ff1822
WEIDMAN, Catherine f1825
WEISENBERGER, George wff1817
WELCH, Jacob f1795
WELLER, George w1849; f1852; f1854; f184
WELLS, Simon f1866
WELSH, Elizabeth wf1879
        Jacob w1778
        John J. ff1849; f1852
        Michael f1827
        Michael f1778; f1827
WELSHANS, Henry w1863
WELSHANCE, Henry f1866
WENDLE, John f1827
        Mary f1827
WENTZ, Harry ff1879
        Henry ff1874
WESTENHAVER, John wfff1852; ff1849
WEVER, C.J. f1879
        Casper wff1879
        Charles J. ff1878
        George S. fff1873
        Joseph ff1827
WHITE, Elizabeth f1842
        John f1822; fff1825; f1827; f1795
WHITENECK, Henry ff1817
WHITING, C.N. ff1846
        Charles H. f1852; f1866
        Charles Henry w1846
        Elizabeth ff1795
        Francis f1778
        Matthew f1791; f1795; f1788
WHITMORE, Frederick f1778
WHITNAH, John C. w1852
WHITSON, Barb ff1879
        William A. w1863
WHITTINGTON, Sarah E. f1852
WIBELEY, C.B. ff1849
WICKERSHAM, Elizabeth f1838
        Eliza f1838; f1843
        Francis f1838
        James f1838
        Jane f1838
        Jonathan w1822; fff1825; f1827
        Nariud? f1827
        Rebecca f1842
        Samuel f1827
WIDDESS, Thomas f1839; ff1842

E, John M. f1874
OX, Homer f1804
, James f1795
N, Nicholas w1843
ERSON, Rebecca f1838
HELM, John wf1825; ff1827
AMS, Barbara fff1832
   Charles f1827
   Charles D. f1831
   Cyrus T. ff1879
   Edward C. w1822; fff1825
   Jerome f1788
   Martha w1831; f1832
IAMSON, David C. f1861
   James D. f1873
   John w1841; ff1843; f1846
   Margaret wf1849
   Mary J. f1873
   Samuel ff1849; f1852
   Samuel D. f1873
IS, Richard w1795
ON, Anna C. f1843
   Elizabeth f1874; f1879
   Elijah ff1827
   Henrietta w1839; f1841; f1846
   Henrietta M. f1843
   Isabella ffff1838; f1843
   Isabella C. f1841
   James wf1812; fff1817; f1827;
      w1832; f1839
   James M. f1841; ff1843; f1846
   John wf1778; w1839; ff1841
   John K. fff1843; f1849
   John P. fff1866; f1874
   Joseph f1778; w1791; f1871
   Lewis T. f1873
   Mary ffff1838; f1843
   Mary C. f1843; f1846; f1839
   Philip P. f1804; ff1812
   Robert w1817
   Samuel w1812; ff1817; w1852
   Samuel K. f1843; fff1827
   Susan C. f1843
   Valentine W. f1873
   William w1839; f1841; ff1846; w1831
   William A. f1843; f1849
   William D. f1873
   William Jr. ff1841; f1843
   William P. f1839
   William Sr. ff1841; f1842; f1843
   Willis A. f1852
ETT, Richard ff1788
ER, James f1832
ING, Alexander wff1804
   James w1804
   John wf1817; ff1821; f1827
   Phoebe fff1827

   Samuel ff1812; ff1839; f1841
WITHEROW, Catherine f1852
   Joseph fff1843; f1846
   William P. f1866
WITHERS, William wf1778
WOLFORD, Martin w1778
WOLGOMOT, David fff1795
   Susanna f1795
WOLFF, Charles f1843
   Charles D. w1832; ff1838
   George w1842; f1846
WOOLF, Henry f1852
WOOD, Israel wf1852
   Richard wff1849
   Robert w1863; fff1873
WOODFORD, Mary w1838
WOODS, Alexander w1832
   Israel f1878
WOODWARD, Howard T.C. f1839
   T.C. f1839
   Thomas f1842
WOOLANS, Jacob wfff1778
WORTHING, Ephraim wf1795
WORTHINGTON, Robert wf1778
WRIGHT, Daniel w1878; f1879
   James ff1832
WYNKOOP, Adrian f1817; f1822
   Garrett f1846
   Sarah f1825
WYSONG, John f1866

YARNELL, Joseph fw1817
YATES, Andrew fw1796
YEATES, Andrew f1817
YINGLING, Mary w1796; f1823
YOEL, Ann Eve w1817; f1819
   Henry fw1779
YONG, Elizabeth w1812
YOUNG, Adam fw1858
   David f1799
   Francis f1823
   Henry f1812
   John f1823
   Nicholas w1796
   Noah w1779

ZEILER, Christian f1812
   Peter ff1789; f1812
ZILER, Margaret f1818
ZIMMERMAN, Adam fw1789
   Catherine fw1818; f1825
   Michael f1812
ZINN, Daniel f1825
ZOLL, John f1878
   Nancy f1878
   Stephen f1873
ZOMBRO (ZUMBER), Peter fw1812
   Eve f1828; f1853; w1857

25

ZORN, John fw1873; f1878
    Nancy f1878

ZUCK, John f1825; f1828
ZUCKMAN, Anthony w1828

The following names were inadvertantly left out at the end of page 16, beginning of pa

PAGE, John f1824; f1829
    Thomas f1812
    Thomas S. f1874
PAINSEL (APINPEL?), T.W. f1849
PAINTER, Jacob w1823; f1825; fff1827; f1829;
      wff1841; f1844; f1854
PALMER, Jacob w1808; fff1825
    Thomas w1795; f1808
    William w1854

Made in the USA
Charleston, SC
12 September 2014